To a wonderful "Prop 8 Warrior,"

Thank you for all that you have done, all that you are now doing, and for all that you will yet do. With much love and appreciation,

President Blickenstaff

If the
SAVIOR
Stood Beside Me

All artwork © Greg Olsen. By arrangement with Greg Olsen Art Publishing Inc., Meridian, Idaho, 83642.
For information on art prints by Greg Olsen, Please contact Greg Olsen Art Publishing Inc. at 1-208-888-2585.

Jacket and book design by Jessica A. Warner, © 2008 Covenant Communications, Inc.

Words to the song "If the Savior Stood Beside Me" copyright © 1991 by Sally DeFord. All rights reserved.

Published by Covenant Communications, Inc.
American Fork, Utah

Printed in China
First Printing: October 2008

15 14 13 12 11 10 09 08   10 9 8 7 6 5 4 3 2 1

ISBN-13: 978-1-59811-602-1
ISBN-10: 1-59811-602-9

If the
SAVIOR
Stood Beside Me

ART BY GREG OLSEN

If the Savior stood beside me, I would walk forever with Him by my side.

I would try
my very hardest
to choose the right
and keep His
commandments.

I would follow
in His footsteps
and do what
He would do.

I would
pour out
my soul to
Him through
words and
song.

If the Savior
stood beside me,
I would welcome Him
to my home to teach
me and my family.

I would
worship Him
as my Lord
and King.

Just as Jesus was baptized,
I would follow His example
and be baptized too.

The Savior's love
makes me feel
new and clean.

He leads
and guides
me with His
gentle hand.

The Savior
loved me enough
to die for me,
so that I might
be forgiven of
my sins.

Because of
what He
did for me,
I can return
to heaven to
live with Him.

He created this
beautiful world
and knows all
His creations.

The Savior
truly knows me.
He understands
my trials and
my fears.

And because
the Savior
stands beside me,
I rejoice.

If the Savior stood beside me, would I do the things I do?

Would I think of His commandments and try harder to be true?

Would I follow His example? Would I live more righteously,

If I could see the Savior standing nigh, watching over me?

If the Savior stood beside me, would I say the things I say?

Would my words be true and kind if He were never far away?

Would I try to share the gospel? Would I speak more reverently

If I could see the Savior standing nigh, watching over me?

He is always near me, though I do not see Him there,

And because He loves me dearly, I am in His watchful care.

So I'll be the kind of person that I know I'd like to be

If I could see the Savior standing nigh, watching over me.

Words and music by Sally DeFord.
Copyright © 1991 by Sally DeFord. All rights reserved.